T0198942

# 111 BITS OF WISDOM TO HELP YOU BECOME A BETTER HUMAN

## JOHN PANZELLA

authorHOUSE®

AuthorHouse™
1663 Liberty Drive
Bloomington, IN 47403
www.authorhouse.com
Phone: 1 (800) 839-8640

Published by AuthorHouse  12/18/2018

ISBN: 978-1-5462-6364-7 (sc)
ISBN: 978-1-5462-6365-4 (e)

Print information available on the last page.

Any people depicted in stock imagery provided by Getty Images are models,
and such images are being used for illustrative purposes only.
Certain stock imagery © Getty Images.

This book is printed on acid-free paper.

This book is dedicated to my "sister-cousin" Lisa, who knows me better than anyone on this planet. And to David, for all the love and for all that you do.

# AUTHOR'S NOTE

**Why 111?** This is not meant to be a complete list. Nor is it an overly-aggressive or taxing list. 111 sounded like the right number to me. That's the simple reason behind the number 111. That, and the number 111 makes me happy, as the first thing that comes to mind when I hear the number 111 is the State Highway in California that runs through Palm Springs. Ah, Palm Springs! I love Palm Springs. One of my favorite places in the United States and home to many dear friends. *(A special shout-out to Gabe and Jim!)*

In these pages, you'll experience simple ***bits of wisdom***, which are lessons that I've learned and words that have been shared with me over the years. Some are words I've either heard or read at different points in my life that have stuck and resonated with me. Some are based on my own conclusions and observations. All are wonderful life lessons. Some lessons I learned the hard way. Several of them took a lot of time for me to really understand and implement. Others were a simple change of pattern or habit. At this stage of my life (51 years old at the time of this book's publication), they're now a natural part of who I am. They are reflected in my spirit as well as my daily actions and outlooks which have, without question, improved the overall quality of my life.

There are several wonderful children and young adults in my everyday life - Lilly, Matthew, Devin, Breighan and Nicholas, to name a few. My hope is that they will take the words contained in this book to heart and incorporate them into their lives much sooner than I did. Wherever their lives may take them, I want the words contained in this book to help, guide and lift them.

And I want this book to help, guide and lift you too. There's nothing more powerful than hearing (or reading) the right words at the right time. Read each page, and then pause. Let the words in. Reflect upon each message. Some messages are simple and straight-forward, some may trigger an eye-roll, some a chuckle, while others are deeper in meaning. Remove any resistance you may have to receiving the message and allow it to become a part of your being so, like me, they can become a natural part of your spirit, outlook and actions.

Personally, I think this book would be a wonderful tool for group discussions, including parent/child discussions, and maybe even for therapy sessions, both formal and informal.

I'm very proud of my first book called *"Give Yourself Some Credit! A Graduate's Guide to Understanding and Establishing Good Credit"* which introduces teens and young adults to the skills and tools associated with building and managing their finances relating to their personal credit. This time around, for my second book *"111 Bits of Wisdom to Help You Become a Better Human"* I'm taking a more philosophical and introspective approach as far as offering advice – while remaining practical.

I'm honored to share this journey with you. And thank you for taking it with me.

All is well.

*John*

Never underestimate the power of the words *"Please"* and *"Thank you."* Use them often and with sincerity.

2

Never argue with fools. You'll never win, and you'll likely become frustrated. Despite what you may have been taught, it's acceptable (and sometimes healthier) not to respond. It's OK to remain silent. It takes strength to step away.

The words *"I'm sorry"* can go a long way. Using them doesn't always mean you're in the wrong. However, if you are in the wrong, say (or write) them with sincerity and do better going forward.

Every time you get behind the wheel, you are taking your passengers, pedestrians, and other drivers' lives and livelihoods into your hands, as well as your own. Driving is a convenience and a privilege; however, don't lose sight of the fact that you're operating a potentially deadly machine.

5

Kindness always matters, whether it's noticed or not.

Your word is your honor. When you give your word, keep it.

Show up. And be on time.

It's OK to ask for help when you need it.

9

As humans, we are more alike than we are different.

Trust life and know that it continues to get better if you want it to.

Everyone gets thrown curve balls, usually when we least expect them. The difference between being harmed and persevering depends on our reactions. Think of life's curve balls as opportunities to reset.

There's a tremendous opportunity in recovery.

Never serve food, or sit for a meal, without a napkin.

You can still love someone and hate their actions. You can still like someone and not like their politics.

Even in nature, no storm lasts forever. The sun is always present behind the dark clouds and sunlight will always prevail. It's just a matter of time.

Guilt is one the worst emotions. Its only job is to inflict pain. Drop guilt from your life. Lose guilt, but don't lose the lesson that may be associated with the situation.

There's a lot that can be learned from nature.
Take time to watch, listen, observe and learn.

Don't wait until you need credit in your name to start building credit.

**19**

Be the neighbor you want to have.

Always trust your instinct.

Your fondest memories will involve the people in your life, not how much money you had at the time.

**Be kind to all animals.**

Invest in a butterfly net with a long handle to trap and release insects when they enter your inside space.

**24**

Vote.

If you use cream and/or sugar in your coffee or tea, consider putting them in the mug first, before the liquid, to eliminate the need for a spoon or stirrer.

Always be a good example for children. Their minds are like sponges and they notice everything.

It's never a bad time or too late to start saving money.

Make your bed every day.

**Don't buy cheap toilet paper.**

Stretch your body - daily.

Laughter is a powerful medicine. Look for reasons to laugh more.

**32**

You'll never please everyone, so don't bother trying.

Take good care of your teeth. Floss. See a dentist
regularly for cleanings and check-ups.

**34**

Know the difference between *Your* and *You're* (you are).

"Narcissism" can be defined as having an excessive or erotic interest in oneself and one's physical appearance. Never date a narcissist.

Strength doesn't have to be bold or loud.

Silence and refrain are often better solutions than engagement that can lead to drama and upset.

**38**

Limit your sugar (and sugar substitute) intake.

Choose an exercise regime that works well for your body, which can change as your body changes. Engage in exercise regularly.

Your ears are sensitive muscles. Don't abuse them by blasting music through your earbuds.

Respect the personal space of others – physically, audibly, and visually.

Always bring a gift for the host or hostess when you're an invited guest.

**Respect R.S.V.P. requests.**

Be more impressed with people who change the world for the better than with celebrities.

**45**

There's nothing more emotionally cleansing than a good cry, for both men and women.

Stay hydrated. Drink lots of water – even in the winter months and during rainy seasons.

**Be humble.**

**48**

Listen to your body. It has a voice of its own.

49

**Trust in Life.**

Learn the art of meditation. Develop a meditation style and frequency that works best for you.

Always be happy for successful people. Allowing positive energy associated with their success will support your success. Everyone has their moment. Let them have theirs and celebrate with them. You will have yours too.

We are in control of our own happiness.

53

Help the less fortunate. Volunteer.

Choose quality over quantity.

Get to know how much sleep your mind and body need to function optimally and strive to achieve it. Fall into a consistent sleep pattern. Never underestimate the power of a good night's sleep.

It's OK to say "No" (or even better – "No, thank you") without explaining yourself.

Live and let live. Yet, do no harm.

Gratitude is the key that unlocks the door to life's treasures. The more thankful you are, even for the smallest things, the more life will respond to you in positive ways.

If you don't pursue what you want, you'll never have it.

**60**

If you never ask the question, the answer will remain unknown.

If you don't take the first step, you'll never move forward.

**62**

Always make eye contact when shaking hands.

Do something today that your future self will thank you for.

**64**

Embrace and celebrate how you're different.

What you give attention to is what what you're inviting (more of) into your life.

*(See #34.)*

**66**

Keep an open mind. Just because you believe something doesn't make it true.

Explore and develop your creative and artistic side.

68

When adopting a pet, remember you're making a commitment that can span many years - even a decade or two.

69

Invest in comfortable bedding, quality bed pillows, and luxurious bath towels.

**70**

Keep a working calendar of your activities, appointments and important birthdays.

Support the Arts. Visit museums and see plays and other live performances.

Your local library has much to offer. Become a member and tap into the free resources that are available to you.

Everything in moderation.

**74**

Each day is a precious gift. Don't squander it.

**75**

Get a passport. Keep it current.

Despite any emotional attachment you may have to one side of anyone's story, it's important to keep in mind that every story has two sides. Sometimes three.

Perform at least one random act of kindness daily.

78

Anger is only one letter short of Danger.

**79**

Success can be defined in many ways and may not necessarily involve money or fame. Create your own definition of success and strive to achieve it.

Let your character and principles define you
more so than your occupation, your family's
dysfunction, your past, or any bad moments you
may have experienced. And may your character
and principles continue to drive your actions
and reactions, especially during moments of
inconvenience.

**81**

Explore the many wonderful types and flavors of tea.

Go easy on yourself. Less pressure. More self-love.

Education does not guarantee intelligence.

Be as forgiving to yourself as others. Be forgiving to others as you are to yourself.

85

The ultimate display of strength is patience.

Never miss an opportunity to pay someone a compliment.

Thinking ahead can save your behind.

Be wary of those who wallow in woes.

**89**

Keep your cellphone out of your hands while driving and while in darkened theaters.

90

Taking a nap is an act of self-care.

Karma always prevails.

Truthfulness is honorable and liberating.

**93**

Put more energy into what's ahead of you rather than what's behind you. You can't drive a car while focusing on the rear-view mirror.

Your wounds, as well as your vulnerabilities, help give birth to your power.

**95**

Miracles happen every day. Be open to miracles
in your life.

**96**

Listen first. Then decide.

Celebrate diversity.

There will always be critics. Learn to stay focused on your intentions, your vision, and moving forward with what feels right for you.

## 99

Travel.

If you haven't worn or used it in a year, then donate it.

**Be open to receiving more than you expect.**

We all have internal "reset" buttons that we need to press every so often to help us restrategize and refresh. And it's perfectly acceptable to use them when needed.

**103**

Happiness is contagious. Spread it!

If you look for trouble, you'll find it. If you look for drama, you'll find that too.

When sitting down for a meal that involves meat, poultry or fish, take a moment to pay a silent blessing for the animal that gave its life for your meal.

Brevity is the essence of effective communication. In other words, keep your messages short and simple.

It is possible to quickly achieve a state of improved happiness by shifting your focus to a good-feeling thought.

Don't watch the evening news, horror movies or anything that might upset you before bedtime. Don't take bad news or dark stories into sleep with you.

If you're looking for that one special person who can change your life for the better, look in the mirror.

Your value does not decrease just because someone is unable or unwilling to see your worth.

Love is always the right answer.

# ABOUT THE AUTHOR

John Panzella 's personal and professional life paths have been enhanced by the people he has met and the lessons he has learned along the way. He is a strong believer in sharing a "good thing" and with his second book, *111 Bits of Wisdom to help you become a Better Human,* he is pleased to be able to share 111 "good things" with his readers. In his spare time, John helps high-school and college students improve their understanding of credit through his seminars and with his first book, *"Give Yourself Some Credit! A Graduate's Guide to Understanding and Establishing Good Credit."* John loves his family, including his three cats. He's a believer and supporter of kindness, self-improvement, and helping to make the world a better place for all. John is a fan of comfortable clothes, gatherings with friends, live theater, and warm tea.

Printed in the United States
By Bookmasters